NEXT TO THE THRONE OF GOD
KOLOB CANYONS, ZION NATIONAL PARK

A SECRET ZION

Think of Zion Canyon. Soaring cathedral walls reach heavenward from the thickly vegetated canyon floor, river-cut, water-shaped — tapering and dimpling as the pale summits break free of the narrows below. Three million people a year crowd along the cool, moist corridors and high peaks at the heart of Zion National Park, seeking an encounter with nature. It is a nurturing landscape, where camaraderie and good spirits are as plentiful as trails. But there is more to Zion — places where fewer visitors tread.

Swing your gaze upward, to where a red-tailed hawk is silhouetted against a bowl-shaped sky. As you look, the great raptor flaps its way up and over the pale rock domes and begins to soar out of sight, toward the backcountry. Imagine for a moment that you too could fly across this great landscape. What would you see? As you leave Zion Canyon and fly in a northwesterly direction, you would find yourself above a wild skyline country of cinder cones, whirling sandstone, evergreen forests, and pale grass pastures flanked by red cliffs. Far below, several backpackers trudge along the lonesome West Rim Trail, as they make their way across the Kolob Terrace, at the center of the 11,000-foot Markagunt Plateau. Scuffling boots startle a jackrabbit from the protective cover of a pinyon tree, and somewhere, in the shadows, a mountain lion patiently scans the horizon in search of prey. The long moan of the wind is a constant companion.

Suddenly, the hikers disappear from view, descending into one of the steep, sandy drainages that eat back the western edge of the plateau — gradually closing the distance between the western desert and Zion Canyon. The landscape dissolves into a convolution of green-topped mesas, dizzying slickrock cliffs, and intersecting creeks. Across La Verkin Creek, 310-foot-long Kolob Arch, perhaps the world's largest rock span, nestles modestly in a side canyon, amid sheltering cliffs — hidden here more than seven miles from Interstate 15. All is quiet, peaceful, harmonious. The only sign of human presence is an occasional derelict cabin or a corral.

On the other side of this creek-cut island of rock, an orange-red sunset skims the Great Basin desert, until its fiery rays hit the 4,000-foot cliffs that mark the boundary between the Colorado Plateau and the Basin and Range province beyond. All at once, the cliffs are infused with color.and a natural landmark of epic proportions is illuminated. Like coastal headlands jutting toward a vast sagebrush ocean, five huge, stubby fingers of salmon-colored sandstone reach westward, their short interstices lined with jewel-green foliage and shadowed alcoves, fissures, and ledges. At the base of the cliffs, a scrub jay chatters to a rock squirrel beneath a

spreading juniper, and a woodpecker makes an answering tap in a pine. Beneath the shady umbrella of a tall cottonwood tree, campers cool their heels in Timber Creek and admire the cliffs. A few miles away travelers pull off the interstate, as they catch sight of the vermilion rocks through a gap in the Hurricane Cliffs. They spill from their vehicles, armed with cameras, exclaiming at the sight. It's a nightly show and one of the best-kept secrets in southern Utah: the Finger Canyons of the Kolob.

WHERE MAN IS BUT A VISITOR

The 30,000 acres that make up the Kolob Canyons unit in northwestern Zion are a special area of the park. Set aside for protection as a national monument in 1937, and added to Zion National Park in 1956, this is one of those coveted places where it is still possible to venture into pristine backcountry and have a secluded wilderness experience. But casual visitors also find much to enjoy: a five-mile, paved scenic drive and two pleasant day-hike trails give an up-close view of the epic geology of the Finger Canyons, without requiring lengthy preparations beforehand.

As you enter Kolob Canyons along the scenic drive, you cross a major fault line, and a host of lesser siblings, all of which gave rise — literally — to the great plateau in which Zion was born. An enormous natural cutaway of the Markagunt Plateau, the spectacular, colorful Finger Canyons display the oldest and youngest rocks in Zion, as well as its tallest peak: 8,926-foot Horse Ranch Mountain.

Peregrine falcons share high cliff ledges with ravens and hawks, Mexican spotted owls find well-hidden roosting sites deep in slot canyons, Douglas fir trees take root in cool exposures across the canyon from desert yucca, Hay's sedges grow alongside columbines and monkeyflowers in hanging gardens at canyon seeps. All find a protected home in the remote, wild Kolob District.

Above: Yuccas provided soap,

....

fibers, and food to native peoples

....

for centuries. Opposite: At

....

8,926 feet high, Horse Ranch

....

Mountain is the highest point

....

in Zion National Park.

....

Overleaf: Creeks carved the

....

high mesas and deep drainages

....

found in Kolob Canyons.

THE ROCKS SPEAK

Above: The juxtaposition of

natural forms provides dramatic

contrast. The deep green needles

of these pine trees are given texture

and heightened color by the red

Navajo Sandstone behind them.

Opposite: Water percolating

through porous sandstone makes

the cliffs unstable, causing numerous

rockfalls during heavy rains.

A drive along the short scenic highway that winds into the Finger Canyons exposes 250 million years of southern Utah geology and ten different rock formations. Where high mountains, forests, rivers, and deserts now dominate, the land was once low and covered with a warm, tropical ocean that lapped here during the Permian age. The tiny shelled creatures that died in this shallow sea built the pale Kaibab Limestone, which makes up the bulk of the towering Hurricane Cliffs behind the Kolob Visitor Center, just off Interstate 15.

In early Triassic times, what had once been a single supercontinent known as Pangaea was pulled apart, as violent movements deep within the earth's crust began to reconfigure its surface. The continents floated like icebergs on a sea of magma, moving position, their climates changing as they entered new latitudes. In the Southwest, the climate dried and the Permian sea receded. Marine sediments began to mix with sediments from seasonal streams that fed into the sea, compacting eventually into the huge beds of pink-, white-, and chocolate-colored Moenkopi shale you see at the Taylor Creek trailhead.

Volcanic activity increased, and dinosaurs evolved and began to populate swamps and streams lined with great conifers and fernlike cycads. As these arboreal giants died, they fell into the streams, formed log jams, and were eventually entombed by mud. Volcanic ash mixed with groundwater and seeped into the buried corpses, replacing woody tissue with colorful silicates. Today, gem-filled petrified wood and uranium is abundant in the Chinle Formation — a blend of soft, multihued mudstones, siltstones, and limestones above the Moenkopi Formation, on display along Taylor Creek.

JURASSIC PARK: Just before you reach Lee Pass, near the end of the scenic drive, the red Moenave and Kayenta siltstones and sandstones that sit directly above the crumbly Chinle come into view. To the left of the road, above the North Fork of Taylor Creek, looms Horse Ranch Mountain, its monolithic sandstone form capped with younger Temple Cap, Carmel, and Dakota formations and very recent basalts. The 8,000-foot plateaus that make up the Finger Canyons of the Kolob are in sight now — Tucupit, Paria, Beatty, Nagunt, and Timber Top mesas — their etched, sandstone facades plunging 2,000 feet to the canyons below.

The Navajo Sandstone is the mother rock to which Zion owes its existence. The Navajo reaches its ultimate expression in the Kolob District, where it is redder and, some say, more beautifully sculpted than even in Zion Canyon. The sandstone was laid down approximately 180 million years ago in a vast Sahara-like desert of blowing sand and cross-bedded dunes up to 3,500 feet high, which spread across parts of seven western states. Very few animals could

tolerate such conditions, and their fossils are almost unknown in this formation. About 20 million years later, when seas and streams once more began to move over the land, depositing the limestones and sandstones of the Carmel Formation, the weight of these deposits began to compress the underlying quartz dunes. In time, they hardened into the 2,000-foot-thick, porous, orange-red Navajo Sandstone, cemented with lime and iron from the overlying formations, which we see today.

SEISMIC ROCK AND ROLL: As the Cretaceous period dawned, about 60 million years ago, the dinosaurs had died out, mammals were assuming dominance, the climate was much drier, and streams and lakes had replaced seas. The final layer of sedimentary rocks in Kolob today, the Dakota Sandstone, was deposited as movement along major faults was again gathering force and changing the topography of the West.

All this was nothing new for the Kolob. At least 100 million years before, a period of powerful east-west compression — dubbed the Sevier Orogeny — produced a great anticline, known as the Kanarra Fold, in the area around Taylor Creek. Here, the Moenave Formation was thrust violently from the east up and over itself, like a large wrinkle in a carpet. Roughly aligned with other anticlines in the vicinity, the east-west–trending faults may have subsequently been occupied by Taylor Creek and other streams, which began to carve the Finger Canyons of the Kolob. When the Rocky Mountains and the mile-high Colorado Plateau were squeezed up, between 80 and 40 million years ago, a network of faults was already in place in the Kolob — all of them ready to spring to life under the right local conditions.

Sometime between 17 and 14 million years ago, the north-south–trending Sevier and Hurricane faults, which sit to the east and west of the Markagunt Plateau respectively, moved violently, perhaps in response to a release of pressure following the building of the Rockies. The Markagunt Plateau was forced 4,000 feet above the low-lying Great Basin desert west of the Hurricane Fault, and other plateaus arose to the east. Powerful volcanic activity continued along the 200-mile-long Hurricane Fault (an extension of the active Wasatch Fault Line) until as recent as 4,000 years ago, dotting the mountain tops with basaltic lava flows and cinder cones. Today, earthquakes rumble regularly through the Zion area, causing vulnerable base rocks such as the Moenkopi and the Chinle to slump or give way and slabs of Navajo Sandstone to crash to the ground. The Kolob is an unstable place; here, the land is dynamic, always shifting and transforming its features. Every visit reveals something new.

Above: Sunset makes the great
....
cliff walls above the South Fork of
....
Taylor Creek glow red at the end
....
of the day. Opposite: Leafy maples
....
shelter in the lee of a colorful
....
canyon wall. Overleaf: The pristine
....
quality of this less visited section of
....
Zion National Park fills the senses.

Above: Water has given shape to

....

Kolob Canyons. Moist, cool mesa tops

....

and deep canyon recesses offer a

....

welcome respite from hot, dry open areas

....

in the canyons. Opposite: Double Arch

....

Alcove was originally named Leda's Cave

....

by the children who lived at the base of

....

the canyon at the turn of the century.

THE FINGER CANYONS APPEAR: Downcutting by existing streams intensified as the plateaus rose. In the Kolob, sediment-laden flashfloods and waterfalls began to carve short canyons and hanging valleys in the Navajo Sandstone. Exposed facades came under attack from temperature extremes, wind, rain, ice, plant roots, and animal activity. The porous Navajo Sandstone is particularly undermined by groundwater percolating down through joints and washing out iron and lime cement, causing the rock to shear away in vertical slabs. In the Kolob, Double Arch Alcove in the Middle Fork of Taylor Creek is a superb example of this type of exfoliating erosion. Under the right conditions, alcoves turn into spans such as Kolob Arch, which sits seven miles away from the road, in the backcountry. The trademark dripping rocks and hanging gardens of Zion also owe their existence to the passage of water through the porous rock. As groundwater reaches the impervious Kayenta shales beneath the Navajo, its downward route is blocked and the water is forced to exit horizontally along springlines, or seeps. The rocks are constantly kept wet and are further darkened by weathering of minerals and bacteria living on the surface, forming a patina known as desert varnish. Until the 1200s, Anasazi Indians hunting here occasionally etched symbols in these darkened surfaces, which can still be faintly seen in places.

Several unusual geological features in the Kolob intrigue researchers. Water erosion generally turns Navajo Sandstone pale and crumbly; but at Kolob, the rocks are uniformly red, despite their high elevation and the leaching action of groundwater. In the 1950s, geologist Herbert Gregory theorized that this may be because the Finger Canyons sit farther west, are more iron-rich, and are possibly lower in the formation as a whole. But the question is still open to speculation.

Frequent landslides in box canyons set up ideal conditions for snowmelt from high plateaus to dam up behind rock chutes into ephemeral lakes and ponds. Sometimes, though, snowmelt is too rapid and the dam breaks suddenly, causing a destructive flashflood. (In the wet spring of 1993, a dam broke in Taylor Canyon and sent a wave of water and debris down the canyon and onto the freeway.) In 1993, a group of geologists began studying Beatty Lake in the South Fork of Taylor Creek to see what it and other lakes reveal about the last 10,000 years. They believe they may have uncovered evidence that the damming material, previously thought to be earthquake-induced rock fall, is in fact a glacial moraine. A permanent pond in Beartrap Canyon may be explained similarly. The coolness of the canyons, and their one-way outlet, gives credence to the notion that remnant glaciers from the last Ice Age may have been present here. Further studies are underway to test this hypothesis.

FROM PLATEAU TO CANYON

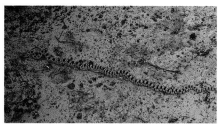

Above: Reptiles like the warm sand

....

and sheltering rocks of Kolob Canyons.

....

This western gopher snake is one of several

....

snakes found here. Opposite: This

....

strawberry cactus enjoys the desert conditions

....

at low elevations. Overleaf: Snow on red

....

sandstone gives a magical quality to the

....

South Fork of Taylor Creek.

Kolob's cliffs, canyons, and creeks offer a range of overlapping habitats. The 8,000-foot plateaus are fairly inaccessible and snow-covered from October to May. Cool-season grasses and lofty, waxy-needled ponderosa pine and fir trees are best suited to this rugged environment. Green leaf manzanita, bigtooth maple, Gambel oak, and rockplant stay low to the ground here, growing alongside woody-stemmed wildflowers, such as Indian paintbrush and delicate penstemons, which enliven bare rock ledges in summer.

From cliff-top eyries, golden eagles, peregrine falcons, and other raptors stay on the look-out for mice, rock squirrels, and other prey. Their neighbors, the hoarse-throated ravens, are much in evidence, swooping around each other in a mating ritual every spring. Timid cougars and bobcats feast on deer during night-time hunts and compete with coyotes and grey foxes for tasty jackrabbits, cottontails, and other burrowers.

Warmer, drier temperatures and sand have created exposed desertlike conditions in the 5,000-foot-elevation canyons. Cheatgrass blows in on the wind and settles in disturbed areas. Narrowleaf yucca, pricklypear cactus, and sagebrush cluster along sandy creek banks beside Zion milkvetch and bladderpod, a species introduced by man. St. George milkvetch and stinking milkvetch prefer the selenium-rich soil of the Moenkopi and Chinle rocks. Pinyon and juniper have commandeered rock ledges and slopes, outcompeting the mountain mahogany, manzanita, and shrub live oak that also like to live here. Watch for reptiles. Canyon treefrogs relish riparian areas, while you may encounter western rattlesnakes, striped whipsnakes, and whiptail lizards along the Taylor Creek Trail and other sandy areas. (Give snakes safe distance; they are as wary of you as you are of them.)

The merry song of the canyon wren reverberates off canyon walls, frequently drowned out by garrulous Steller's and pinyon jays squabbling with rock squirrels over who gets the nuts and seeds. At creek's edge, water-loving cottonwoods sink down thirsty roots, and occasionally ponderosas or junipers thrive in the protected drainages. At night, high-country dwellers come to the water to drink, leaving their distinctive prints in damp sand. In the fall, tarantulas can be seen crossing the road in pursuit of a mate.

Deeper in the canyons, where sunlight rarely reaches, birch trees, colorful bigtooth maples, and firs are surprising lowland residents. The cool, damp conditions also foster hanging gardens of monkeyflower, columbine, maidenhair fern, Zion daisy, Zion shooting star, Hay's sedge, and butterfly milkweed — some found only in Zion, others common in wetlands throughout the Southwest.

Hardly a Human Footprint

The Kolob has seen humans come and go for millennia, but few remained in these rugged canyons for long. Anasazi Indians, and later Paiute nomads, ventured in seasonally to hunt bighorn sheep, deer, elk, rabbits, and the occasional bear or mountain lion in the high country, and to harvest yucca pods, roots, and threads, pinyon nuts, grass seed, and other wild foods as summer turned to autumn. It is said that Taylor Creek was known as "Brother-in-Law Stream" by the Paiutes, for the related family groups that camped there. Tucupit Point carries the Paiute name for wild cat; Paria Point may refer to elk; Nagunt Mesa apparently echoes the Paiute word for bighorn sheep, *naga*. The Paiutes who live nearby still refer to Kolob as a spiritual place, where they could seek physical and emotional sustenance.

The Mormons, who arrived in the area in 1852, were also impressed by the beauty of the Finger Canyons and the abundant grazing for their livestock. They named the area *Kolob*, which in their scripture means "the star closest to the throne of God." They built the pioneer settlement of Fort Harmony just to the west, where they grew crops and corralled their livestock.

They were led by the infamous John D. Lee, who, in 1857, was implicated in the tragic Mountain Meadows Massacre. Almost an entire party of California-bound emigrants was murdered at nearby Mountain Meadows, a popular rest stop on the Old Spanish Trail, during a time of enormous tensions between the federal government and Utah's Mormons. Lee's diaries indicate that he initially hid out in the Kolob and built a cabin in Cane Hollow, a remote drainage. He established a trail that, in the space of a day, allowed him to travel between the village of Virgin and the cliffs overlooking Fort Harmony, where he could keep watch over the family home. The trail was well known to local Mormons, who used it for many years as a shortcut. A second Lee Cabin apparently existed just north of Taylor Creek, but is now in ruins. Lee hid in remote areas of southern Utah and northern Arizona for twenty years, but was eventually captured at Panguitch, just to the northeast. He was executed by the government at the site of the massacre in Mountain Meadows in 1877. Lee Pass is named for this Mormon pioneer.

Farming and some ranching continued in the Kolob until the mid-1930s. In 1921, the Pollock family built a cement house at the mouth of Taylor Creek (then called Dry Creek) and raised sheep, pigs, chickens, cattle, and some crops. In 1915, the twelve Pollock children had ventured up the canyon and found Double Arch Alcove, which they named Leda's Cave, in honor of the eldest child. The children's father often frightened the children with stories about Crackfoot the Bear, a bear with an injured paw that lived in Dry Creek Canyon.

A hike along the Middle Fork of Taylor Creek takes you past Palmer, Fife, and Larson cabins, built by those families in 1929 and 1930. Lumbering and grazing had so denuded the

Above: Mule deer are seen at all
....
elevations in Kolob Canyons, where they
....
form the diet of rarely seen mountain lions.
....
Opposite: Pricklypear cactus bloom
....
in dry, sheltered locations in spring.
....
By summer, they sport tasty red fruits.

Above: The backcountry of

....

Kolob Canyons is managed by the

....

National Park Service as wilderness.

....

It is still possible to get away

....

from it all in this remote area.

canyon that the families decided instead to rest the land by doing small-scale farming and by hosting summer geology and photography trips from nearby Cedar City. Arthur Fife taught at the Branch Agricultural College in Cedar City (now Southern Utah University). The families moved when the monument was set aside.

Today, a few ranch inholdings still exist on the plateaus, though the days of the annual cattle drive down La Verkin Creek are over. Grazing continues outside the park on the Kolob Terrace, but of more concern now are the impacts of increased use of the backcountry and new construction on park borders, which threatens drainages and wildlife in the park, including two endangered species.

Henry David Thoreau said: "In wilderness is the preservation of the world." And, despite the threat of modern encroachments, Kolob remains an island of serenity — its geological beauty and natural riches one of the high points of a visit to Zion National Park. Thoreau would have been well pleased.

VISITOR INFORMATION

Above: Kolob Arch, with a span

. . . .

of 310 feet, is possibly the longest

. . . .

known arch in the southwest.

Most of the Kolob Canyons area is proposed wilderness and has been managed as such for the nearly sixty years since the area received federal protection. As a result, much of the backcountry must be explored on foot or on horseback. The 5.2-mile paved scenic drive, just off Interstate 15, offers an excellent overview of the geology of the Finger Canyons. Three trailheads are located along the drive, and a day picnic area is located at the turnaround. There is no gas, food, or lodging in this part of the park. The nearest services are located in Cedar City, twenty miles north on Interstate 15.

HIKING: There are only two designated day trails in the Finger Canyons area: the 1-mile Timber Creek Overlook Trail, which leaves from the picnic area at the end of the scenic drive and offers wonderful views of the Kolob backcountry to the south, and the 5.4-mile roundtrip Middle Fork of Taylor Creek Trail, which takes you past two homestead cabins and beneath Double Arch Alcove to the place where Paria and Beatty points meet. But many other hiking possibilities exist in the backcountry. It's a strenuous 14.4-mile roundtrip hike to Kolob Arch, which is best done overnight. The trail leaves from Lee Pass Trailhead, takes you through Timber Creek to its junction with La Verkin Creek, and on to the arch. The Hop Valley Trail continues westward out of the drainage, through Hop Valley and up to Lava Point, where you can shuttle back along the Kolob Road or continue hiking the West Rim Trail to Zion Canyon. You may also choose to hike farther into the La Verkin Creek drainage and explore the stunning country beyond the Kolob Arch. All overnight stays in Zion National Park require a permit.

CAMPING: Primitive camping is allowed only at designated locations in the backcountry, and all wilderness rules apply. Bring plenty of water, water purification tablets, adequate food supplies, and protective clothing and skin care. Temperatures (Fahrenheit) in winter stay below freezing at night and may only reach the 50s in the day. Snow is often present, even in the lower elevations, until April. In summer, temperatures climb into the 90s, and severe thunderstorms and flashfloods can appear abruptly. Hikers in the Kolob Canyons need to pay particular attention to changing conditions and beware of flashfloods and rockfalls. Discuss your plans with rangers before setting out.

The Kolob Visitor Center, just east of Interstate 15, is open 9 A.M. to 4:30 P.M. (longer hours in summer). It offers a ranger-staffed information counter, exhibits about the Kolob, and a well-stocked bookstore. For more information, write: Superintendent, Zion National Park, Springdale, Utah 84767-1099.   Tel: 801-586-9548.

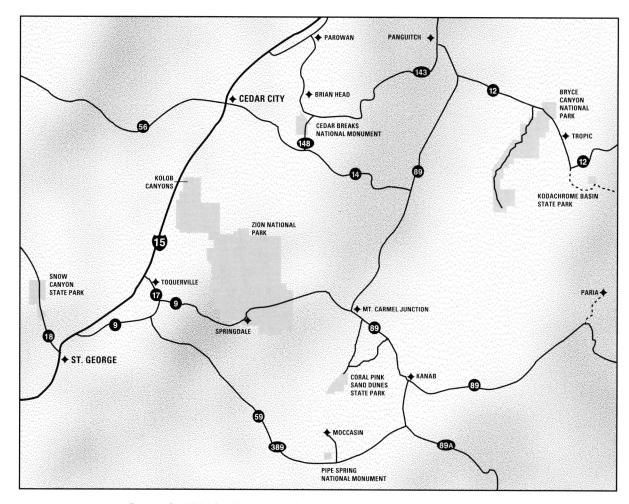

©1994 Photography by Gail Bandini (p. 17, 20, 21), Lynn Chamberlain (p. 9, 22),
Carr Clifton (p. 14), Clint Crawley (front cover, p. 4, 5, 6/7, 16),
Brian Hopkins/National Park Service (p. 23), George H. H. Huey (p. 11, 18/19),
Dave Pettit (back cover), Ed Riddell (p. 2, 8, 10), Tom Till (p. 1, 3, 15), and Brad Wagner (p. 12/13)

Written by Nicky Leach   Edited by Rose Houk

Designed by Lee Riddell & Laura Quinlivan   Map Illustrated by Magda Dukeland

Project Coordinated by Jamie Gentry

Printed by Paragon Press, Salt Lake City, Utah

ZION NATURAL HISTORY ASSOCIATION